THE
ATTACK
on
PEARL HARBOR

A HISTORY PERSPECTIVES BOOK

Katherine Krieg

Published in the United States of America by Cherry Lake Publishing
Ann Arbor, Michigan
www.cherrylakepublishing.com

Consultants: Peter C. Vermilyea, Lecturer, History Department, Western
Connecticut State University; Marla Conn, ReadAbility, Inc.
Editorial direction: Red Line Editorial
Book design and illustration: Sleeping Bear Press

Photo Credits: Library of Congress, cover (left), 1 (left), 20; Dan
Simonsen/Shutterstock Images, cover (middle), 1 (middle), 18; Robert
Kradin/AP Images, cover (right), 1 (right), 25; Howard R. Hollem/Library
of Congress, 4; AP Images, 6, 11, 14, 16, 22, 23, 28, 30; U.S. Navy/AP
Images, 13

Copyright ©2014 by Cherry Lake Publishing
All rights reserved. No part of this book may be reproduced or utilized in
any form or by any means without written permission from the publisher.

Library of Congress Cataloging-in-Publication Data
Krieg, Katherine.
  The attack on Pearl Harbor / Katherine Krieg.
    pages cm. – (Perspectives library)
  Includes index.
  ISBN 978-1-62431-413-1 (hardcover) – ISBN 978-1-62431-489-6 (pbk.)
– ISBN 978-1-62431-451-3 (pdf) – ISBN 978-1-62431-527-5 (ebook)
 1. Pearl Harbor (Hawaii), Attack on, 1941–Juvenile literature. I. Title.
D767.92.K75 2013
940.54'26693–dc23
                        2013006435

Cherry Lake Publishing would like to acknowledge the work of
The Partnership for 21st Century Skills. Please visit *www.p21.org*
for more information.

Printed in the United States of America
Corporate Graphics Inc.
July 2013
CLFA11

TABLE OF CONTENTS

In this book, you will read about the attack on Pearl Harbor from three perspectives. Each perspective is based on real things that happened to real people who were in or near the attack. As you'll see, the same event can look different depending on one's point of view.

1

Ronald Carter

U.S. Marine

I wince as a nurse cleans the burns on my arm. I'm on board the hospital ship *Solace*, with about 100 other wounded marines and sailors. The ship has also picked up many dead bodies. I'm a U.S. marine stationed at the Pearl Harbor base off the coast of Oahu, Hawaii. It is Sunday, December 7, 1941, and today my country was attacked.

The morning started like any other Sunday. I got out of bed aboard the USS *Arizona*, which was docked on the east side of Ford Island. I had been training on the ship since February 1941. The USS *Arizona* was part of the United States' Pacific **Fleet**, an impressive group of great battleships. This fleet is the country's main military force in the Pacific Ocean.

Other ships were docked with us on Ford Island, including the USS *Nevada* to the east and the USS *West Virginia* and USS *Tennessee* to the west. This grouping of docked ships was called Battleship Row. There were a few other battleships on the west side of Ford Island too, including the USS *Utah* and the USS *Raleigh*.

Europe is at war, and some areas of Asia have also been affected by the conflict. China in particular has been facing danger as Japan tries to conquer more of China's land. On September 27, 1940, Japan joined in the Tripartite Pact with Germany and Italy. The pact linked these countries together as the Axis Powers.

The Axis Powers are fighting against the Allies, mainly Great Britain and France, attempting to gain more land and resources. Great Britain is a major ally to the United States and had been asking for help. But most people in the United States wanted to stay out of the war.

▲ *In 1940, Japan, Germany, and Italy formed the Axis Powers and fought allies of the United States, but the United States still stayed out of the war at that time.*

Before today, my fellow trainees and I thought we were pretty safe at Pearl Harbor. The U.S. military knew that an attack on this base would have to come from Japan, the nearest physical enemy to Hawaii. But they did not think Japan had enough resources to pull off an extensive attack. It was believed that Japanese military forces were already stretched too thin as they tried to expand their rule in East Asia. Plus, we thought the Japanese had simple planes and unskilled pilots. After what I've seen today, I know that's not true.

THINK ABOUT IT

▶ Read Private Carter's explanation of the situation in Europe and Asia. What is the main point? Give two reasons why you think this.

The attack started when I was in the dining hall for breakfast. Since it was Sunday, there were fewer men on the ship. A lot of the crew had weekend passes and were on the main island with their families. As I finished my breakfast, I was startled by the sounding of the ship's siren. The siren calls marines to their anti-aircraft battle stations. These marines operate guns that can bring down enemy aircraft. I thought it was just a drill. By this time, it was close to 8:00 a.m.

As I got closer to the deck, I could hear other marines yelling orders. I knew something was wrong. Then, I was startled by a blast so loud and so near that it shook the whole ship. We were under attack.

I jumped onto the deck to a horrific sight. Japanese **torpedo planes** were zipping through the sky, flying so low I could see some of the pilots' faces. I could tell it was the Japanese because of the red circle painted on the side of each plane.

Men were at their anti-aircraft stations shooting at the enemy planes. The sound of machine guns ripped at the air as our men returned fire. Smoke rose from the battleships around us. Many other ships in the harbor were already smoldering.

HITTING THE AIRFIELDS FIRST

Before bombing the ships anchored on Battleship Row, the Japanese hit U.S. military airfields on Ford Island. Many aircraft were destroyed when they were sitting on the airfields, unaware that the attack was coming. It was an attempt by the Japanese to prevent an American counterattack to protect the ships. But most of the aircraft were away from the harbor at that time. The aircraft that were not destroyed would be incredibly important to the United States' effort in the war. After attacking the airfields, the Japanese launched their attack on the battleships.

I was turning to go below deck for more ammunition when I saw something hurtling toward our ship from above. The Japanese had **bomber planes** flying above their torpedo planes. The bomb

SECOND SOURCE

▶ Find a second source that describes what it was like to be on a ship in Pearl Harbor while it was attacked. Compare the information there to the information in this source.

fell right over the mast of the ship and exploded as it made contact. It sounded like thousands of fireworks going off at once. I saw men near the explosion thrown off the ship completely. The whole ship was on fire in an instant, and flames and burning embers were raining down on us all.

"Abandon ship!" men were yelling as I raced across the deck to the ship's edge, dodging flying debris. My skin felt like it was burning from the heat of the blast. The ship was already sinking so fast I didn't have to jump off. I just stepped out into the water. Swimming wasn't easy. My arm was badly burned. Some water to my left was ablaze, probably due to an oil slick.

Many of the men who abandoned ship with me were too injured to swim to safety, and they drowned.

Many others went down with the ship, trapped in its lower **compartments**. I was lucky. A rescue ship pulled me from the water as I struggled to swim away from the burning USS *Arizona*. Then, I was transferred to *Solace* for first aid.

On *Solace,* I've been hearing more about the attack. The USS *Arizona* was one of many destroyed

▲ *The USS* Arizona *was hit by a bomb and sunk into Pearl Harbor.*

and damaged ships. On our side of Ford Island, torpedo planes did damage to the USS *California*, the USS *Nevada*, the USS *Oklahoma*, and the USS *West Virginia*. Torpedo planes also attacked the west side of Ford Island, hitting the USS *Helena*, USS *Utah*, and USS *Raleigh*. Torpedo attacks were followed up with bomb attacks, like the one that sunk my ship.

That was just the first wave of the attack. The Japanese planes did another sweep over Battleship Row. They attacked some of the ships they had already damaged, making the situation worse. They even bombed some of the ships that were in **dry dock**. They also chased down the USS *Nevada* as it was trying to escape out of the harbor to sea.

This attack nearly destroyed our Pacific Fleet. It is a huge loss for our Pacific forces. It will be a long time before the Pacific Fleet is rebuilt to its original glory. Now, all I can do is sit and wait. I feel certain the United States will declare war on Japan after this.

The Japanese attacked our country without declaring war first. It was a sneak attack, evil and unprovoked. We did not deserve this.

▲ *The Japanese attack damaged or destroyed many U.S. ships.*

2

Ishi Tanaka

Japanese Fighter Pilot

I fly a high-level bomber plane for my country, Japan. Today I helped carry out a surprise attack on the Pearl Harbor base in Oahu, Hawaii.

My country had good reasons to attack Pearl Harbor. The United States placed an oil **embargo** on Japan on July 26, 1941. Because Japan is a small island with limited natural resources, it needs to **import** some resources from other countries. Other countries joined the embargo, and soon Japan lost 88 percent of its imported oil. Cutting off our resources hurt our country. It also affected our government's plans to expand Japanese rule throughout East Asia. Japan could not succeed without these resources. We had to fight back.

Our military was also worried that the United States' Pacific Fleet could get in the way of our efforts to take over more of East Asia. Now that we have attacked their fleet, we hope that the war will be limited, and that any counterstrikes from the United States will be useless.

Preparation for the attack on Pearl Harbor began several weeks ago. Finally our fleet of aircraft carrier ships left Japan on November 27, 1941. Some

SECOND SOURCE

► Find another source that discusses the embargo that the United States placed on Japan prior to the attack on Pearl Harbor. Compare the information here to the information in that source.

of our submarines left ahead of us on November 16.
We had six aircraft carriers in all. Together they
carried more than 420 planes. Battleships and tanker
ships joined the fleet, carrying the fuel we'd need for
the attack. Vice Admiral Chuichi Nagumo is in charge
of commanding these ships.

▲ *Chuichi Nagumo commanded the Japanese attack on Pearl Harbor.*

When I left Japan, no one knew if we would actually attack the United States. **Negotiations** were still going on with the country. The attack could be called off at any time, and we'd have to turn around and go back.

On the early morning of December 7, we got the orders to prepare for the attack. I knew this meant that we were at war with the United States. The aircraft carriers were approximately 300 miles from Pearl

BELIEVED TO BE AT WAR

When the Japanese attacked Pearl Harbor, most Japanese pilots believed their country was already at war with the United States. Striking an enemy before war is declared is against Japanese cultural values and customs.

Harbor when our first planes took off for the attack. My high-level bomber plane was one of the 180 aircraft in the attack's first wave. Torpedo planes and other dive-bombers and fighter planes joined us. We flew for nearly two hours before reaching the harbor.

It was important that the attack be a surprise. Pearl Harbor had many dangerous battleships,

▲ *Japanese planes led the attack on Pearl Harbor.*

submarines, and aircraft. If they knew an attack was coming, we could be in trouble.

As my plane approached Pearl Harbor, I breathed a sigh of relief. The harbor looked almost motionless below us. It was clear the Americans had not heard of our plan to attack. I also was relieved to see so many U.S. battleships anchored at Pearl Harbor. There was a chance that they could have been out at sea.

As a high-level bomber, my job is to drop bombs from my plane, high in the sky. I was anxious and excited. Japanese torpedo planes buzzed under my plane as my crew and I located the targets and dropped bombs on U.S. battleships. It was immediately clear that this attack was a success. I was proud of the strength of my country.

But I was also saddened to think of my **comrades** dying for

ANALYZE THIS

▶ Analyze this account of the attack on Pearl Harbor. How is it different from the account by the U.S. marine? How is it similar?

our country as they attacked the harbor. Even though the attack was a surprise, it was still a very dangerous mission. I knew it was foolish to think we could escape without any casualties on our side.

▲ *Japan's attack caused extensive damage to the United States' Pacific Fleet.*

One part of the attack was not a success. We had hoped that U.S. aircraft carriers would be in the harbor. Our goal had been to destroy as many of the U.S. military aircraft on those carriers as we could. But we did not see the amount of aircraft we were expecting.

Still, the damage we did to the Pacific Fleet was widespread. Overall, the attack was a great victory for Japan. Although I am fearful of the challenges ahead, I am confident that we will succeed in this war.

Alani Onakea

Hawaiian Worker

I'm a native Hawaiian, and my family has lived on the island of Oahu for generations. I live and work in Pearl City, right near the harbor. Yesterday, on December 7, 1941, I had to take cover in my home as the Japanese attacked our island.

Today, December 8, I listened to the radio to hear President Franklin D. Roosevelt give a speech about the attack. In his speech, Roosevelt asked Congress to declare war on Japan. Just 33 minutes later, Congress approved Roosevelt's declaration of war. Our country is now at war, and I am deeply saddened. But I think after this attack, we had no other options.

For about ten years, the United States' relations with Japan have been getting worse. Japan took over

▲ On December 8, 1941, President Roosevelt spoke to a joint session of Congress, urging them to declare war on Japan.

Manchuria, a region that had belonged to China, in 1931. The United States is an ally of China. So, we were even more concerned when Japan tried to take over another part of China in 1937.

In 1940, Japan joined the Axis Powers with Nazi Germany, another enemy of the United States. The United States has been giving aid and weapons to China to help them fight the Japanese invasion.

But I think the thing that must have really made the Japanese angry was when the United States stopped exporting oil and other materials to Japan. Since Japan is an island, they were pretty dependent on these imports from the United States.

Despite all this, the United States had been trying to stay out of the war. We all thought of it as

ANALYZE THIS

▶ How is this perspective on the situation with Japan after the attack on Pearl Harbor different from the perspective of the Japanese pilot? How are the two perspectives similar?

a European war that really didn't have much to do with the United States. There was a lot of pressure for the United States to get involved though. Great Britain has really been struggling as they fight against Nazi Germany. The United States is a key

▲ *Many Americans learned of the Pearl Harbor attack on December 8.*

THINK ABOUT IT

▶ Determine the main point of this paragraph. Pick out one piece of evidence that supports the main point.

ally of the British. We had supplied some resources, including weapons, to help them. Britain is hoping for more, but the United States did not see this war as our battle to fight.

The attack on Pearl Harbor was terrible. It lasted only two hours and 20 minutes. But in that time, 18 of our great battleships were destroyed or damaged. More than 300 aircraft were ruined or damaged. The worst disaster happened on the USS *Arizona*. The Japanese dropped a 1,760-pound bomb on the ship early in the attack. Of the 1,400 men aboard the ship, 1,177 men **perished**. Altogether, more than 2,300 people died in the attack.

Now that we have joined World War II, I am fearful for how this war will affect my family. I am afraid there will be another attack on our harbor.

Since the attack yesterday, our city has been placed under martial law. That means the military is in charge of enforcing laws instead of the police. There are scheduled blackouts every night starting at 6:00 p.m. In a blackout, we have to turn off most of the lights in our homes and draw the shades. This is to make the city look dark so that bomber planes will have a harder time finding targets.

MEMORIALS

Pearl Harbor is now home to many memorials and museums that honor those who died during the attack. The most well-known memorial is the USS *Arizona* Memorial, which is formally called the World War II Valor in the Pacific National Monument. It consists of a 184-foot structure built over the remains of the sunken battleship.

There is talk of everyone needing to carry identification cards to prove that they are not spies for the Japanese. I've also heard that Japanese-run businesses may be shut down. Some people are

▲ *Once the United States declared war on Japan and entered World War II, U.S. troops were sent abroad to fight in the war.*

afraid to trust anyone who is of Japanese descent. But this is a very sad and unfair thing for the more than 150,000 Japanese living here in Hawaii. I know these people are loyal Americans.

I fear what the future may bring. Our army is strong, but the Axis Powers have already advanced so far. Will we be able to help stop them?

LOOK, LOOK AGAIN

This image shows the USS *Arizona* sinking into Pearl Harbor. Use this photograph to answer the following questions:

1. How would a U.S. marine at Pearl Harbor react to this image? What would a U.S. marine say about this image when discussing the attack with his friends back home?

2. How would a Japanese fighter pilot at Pearl Harbor describe this scene to his family in Japan?

3. How would a Hawaiian worker describe this scene to his or her friends? What would a Hawaiian worker think after seeing this image?

GLOSSARY

bomber plane (BAH-mer PLAYN) a plane that attempts to drop a bomb directly on or near enough to damage a target

compartment (kuhm-PAHRT-muhnt) a separate part of a container, where things can be kept away from others

comrade (COM-rad) a friend, usually within the armed forces

dry dock (DRYE DAHK) a dock kept dry for use during construction or repair of ships

embargo (em-BAHR-goh) a government order preventing the shipment of some resources to another country or area

fleet (FLEET) a group of naval ships

import (IM-port) to bring in goods from another country

negotiation (ni-goh-shee-AYE-shuhn) a discussion made in hopes of reaching an agreement or bargain

perish (PERish) to die or to be destroyed

torpedo plane (tor-PEE-doh PLAYN) a plane that drops a torpedo in the water in the direction of the target so the torpedo will propel itself into the target

LEARN MORE

Further Reading

Dougherty, Steven. *Pearl Harbor: The U.S. Enters World War II.* New York: Franklin Watts, 2010.

Gorman, Jacqueline Laks. *Pearl Harbor: A Primary Source History.* Pleasantville, NY: Gareth Stevens, 2009.

McGowen, Tom. *The Attack on Pearl Harbor.* New York: Children's Press, 2007.

Web Sites

"Day of Infamy"—December 7th, 1941
http://library.umkc.edu/spec-col/ww2/pearlharbor/ph-txt.htm
At this Web site, readers can listen to radio broadcasts recorded during the attack on Pearl Harbor.

Remembering Pearl Harbor
http://education.nationalgeographic.com/education/multimedia/interactive/pearl-harbor/?ar_a=1
This Web site includes an interactive map that shows how the attack on Pearl Harbor took place.

INDEX

ABOUT THE AUTHOR

Katherine Krieg is the author and editor of many fiction and nonfiction books for young people.